Selling to the
VP of NO.

by Dave Gray

A note about gender and pronouns.

Unfortunately, it's difficult to write about people in the English language without being gender-specific. Also, since a single main character makes most of the points in the book, I had a difficult choice to make: either choose a gender or create a vague and genderless being called "Pat," "Chris" or "Terry." Neither of these options being attractive, I chose to make the main character male and refer to him consistently as such. Rest assured, Selling Stars and VPs of NO come in both genders. If you would like to see another version of this book with the VP of NO portrayed as a woman, drop us a line. What the market demands, we will deliver.

Why read this book?

You're reading this book because you want somebody to do something. You want him to buy your product, invest in your idea, give you a raise or increase your budget. And he doesn't want to.

In short, you need to learn—Selling: the art of getting someone from "NO" to "GO." This book will share secrets from some of the world's most successful salespeople. But there are a few things it will not do.

It will not show you how to manipulate people against their will.

It will not show you how to sell someone something they don't want, or how to get people to do things that are not in their best interest.

It will not show you how to use pressure, guilt, or emotional manipulation to get what you want.

But if you truly have something valuable to offer, this book will show you how to break through the wall of indifference. When people understand you, they will buy your product, invest in your idea, give you that raise or increase your budget. And you will be a Selling Star.

Selling is hell!

It's the only way to quickly move people from indecision to action. It's also one of the hardest things in the world to do well.

Why is selling so hard? Because at its heart, selling is about change, and most people don't want to change. Change is difficult. It requires them to think, pulls them out of their routine, and forces them to learn new ways of doing things. Change is also a big risk. If they start doing things differently, how do they know it will work? What if it doesn't?

People have lots of strategies for avoiding new ideas. They can be skeptical, dismissive, impatient, rude, inattentive, apathetic or disinterested. You might find it impossible to get an appointment with them. Even if you do, the most obvious and rational arguments may fail to convince them to act.

Deep down, people also know that change is often necessary, even inevitable. But because it makes them uncomfortable, most of them will put it off as long as possible.

Your prospect

Your prospect can get you the result that you want by picking up the phone, waving his hand, or signing a piece of paper. How can you overcome his reluctance and resistance to change? First, forget everything you *think* you know about sales. You can't win by manipulating people or tricking them into buying.

If you're a Selling Star, people will act according to your agenda. But they won't do it because you want them to. They will do it because it is in their best interest. They will do it because it will benefit them. Because it will help them get what they want.

Your prospect, not you, will make the final decision about whether to act or not. Remember, nobody wants to be sold anything! But people do buy things, all the time. Your prospect will buy when he is convinced it is the right thing to do.

Which brings us to Selling Star principle number one: Think like a buyer. Treat your prospect like you would want him to treat you if you were in his position. Look at things from his perspective. Get inside his head, and you won't go wrong.

The WHODO

Before we begin, take a minute to think about what you want to achieve.

WHO are you talking to? This is your prospect, the person who, by direct action, can get you the result that you want.

What do you want him to DO? This is your call to action – the single, specific action you want him to take. The action should be the first decisive step in the selling process. It could be the agreement to proceed – but if you are selling something complex, it may also be simply that your prospect agrees to a meeting.

If you have a specific situation in mind as you read, you will put these ideas into action more quickly. Open the fold-out worksheet in the back of this book, and fill in the WHO and DO blanks before proceeding.

Example:

WHO: My prospect is: A busy executive that never seems to have enough time

DO: My call to action is: Sign up for a seminar on time management

Listening

Selling Stars know how to listen. They ask
questions until they gain a deep and textured
understanding of their prospect's situation. An
intellectual understanding is not enough. Selling
Stars listen until they feel what the prospect
feels. They empathize.

As you talk to prospects, keep checking to
confirm that you have understood correctly. The
more questions you ask, the less tempted you
will be to preach or prescribe solutions. How
would you feel if your doctor prescribed
medication before asking you about your
symptoms? The more your prospect talks to you,
the more he will feel understood, and the more
he will like you. **Selling Star principle number
two: Listen to learn.** Diagnose before you
prescribe. You will be amazed at the results.

Opening and closing

There are two primary ways to approach prospects. Selling Stars understand the difference, and know how to use each method appropriately.

Opening is just what it sounds like — it's a beginning. To open a prospect is to open his mind, to get him thinking, to provoke thought and generate new ideas. Opening is a way to create a comfortable environment and make a person feel understood, so he will be receptive to your thoughts, and hear what you have to say. It opens his mind to possibilities — including the possibility of action.

Closing is the opposite, and, like it sounds, it's about bringing things to a conclusion. Closing is about asking for — and getting — firm commitments. Closing moves your prospect from "thinking" mode into "doing" mode. People are ready to act when they have convinced themselves that the action is appropriate, necessary, right and urgent — and that it must happen NOW.

Both opening and closing are fundamental to successful selling, but if they happen at the wrong time or in the wrong order the result can be disastrous. Selling Star principle number three: Open by opening, close by closing.

How to ask questions

Questions come in two types.

Open questions provoke dialogue. They begin: *"What"* *"How," "Who," "Where,"* or *"Why."* Open questions can never be answered "yes" or "no."

"What area do you think needs the most improvement?"

"How do you do it today?"

"Who will make the final decision?"

"Where are the biggest problem areas?"

"Why hasn't this been done before?"

Closed questions confirm your understanding or seek commitment. They begin: *Do, So, Is, Are, If, Can, Will, Would, Should,* or *Could.* Closed questions can only be answered "yes" or "no."

Some closed questions confirm understanding:

"*Do* you find this acceptable?"

"*So* you think the situation is deteriorating, is that right?"

"*Is* this common?"

"*Are* you saying that these kinds of initiatives have failed in the past?"

Other closed questions seek a commitment:

"*If* I guaranteed immediate delivery, would you buy now?"

"*Can* you think of a reason not to do this?"

"*Will* you decide by Tuesday?"

"*Would* you like this today?"

"*Should* we talk to your boss?"

"*Could* we call him now?"

Ask good questions, for good reasons. Selling Star principle number four: Master the art of asking.

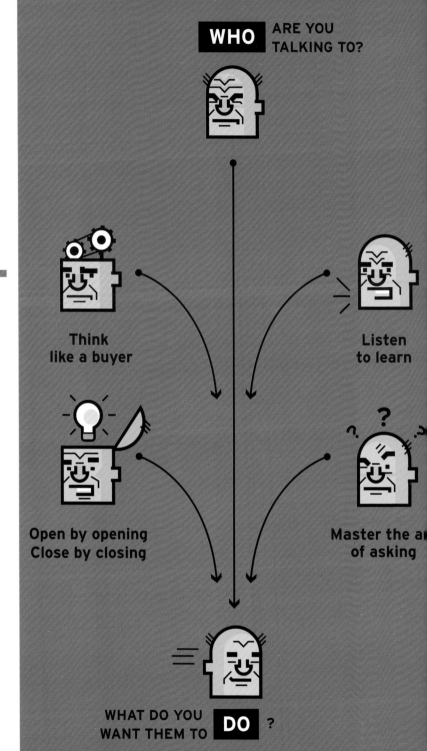

WHO ARE YOU TALKING TO?

Think
like a buyer

Listen
to learn

Open by opening
Close by closing

Master the a[...]
of asking

WHAT DO YOU
WANT THEM TO **DO** ?

Review

Now that you understand the WHODO:

WHO you are talking to, and

What you want him to DO

and the four Selling Star principles:

Think like a buyer

Listen to learn

Open by opening, close by closing

Master the art of asking

It's time to meet your prospect, the VP of NO.

WHY SHOULD I CARE?

The VP of NO

Meet the VP of NO. Every hour of every day, someone tries to sell him something. He has a simple strategy for dealing with these requests: He just says "NO." He figures that people probably want to sell him something he doesn't really need. After all, if he needed it he would already have bought it! And most of the time, he's right.

"Don't call us, we'll call you," he says.

The VP of NO has one simple question that must be answered before he will give you more than a few seconds of his precious time. Whether he explicitly says it or not, that question is always the same:

"Why should I care?"

He needs a reason to listen to you, and there is only one way to get his attention: You must make him uncomfortable. His safe, secure, comfortable position needs to start feeling less safe.

NO is the comfort zone.

Nobody will deny that taking action involves risk. But don't forget, inaction is also risky business: Just ask the guy who didn't steer the Titanic away from the iceberg.

Define the comfort zone

When you enter into a conversation with your prospect, he doesn't start from ground zero – he's not a blank slate for you to write your ideas on. He's a human being, with his own ideas and his own ways of doing things, thank you very much. And he's doing pretty well so far, without any help from you.

There is something that you want your prospect to DO. Something new. He doesn't do it today, or you wouldn't need to convince him of anything. Saying yes to you will force him to change his life in some way. There is something he will have to do differently.

How does he do it today? Why does he do it that way? That's what we call his comfort zone, and you need to get him out of it.

On your worksheet, define your prospect's comfort zone.

Example:

WHAT does he do today? He reacts to events and emergencies as they occur, rather than prioritizing what's important to him and planning his time accordingly.

WHY does he do it that way? He has become dependent on the emergencies, because he feels important and needed when he can resolve a crisis situation.

GO TO THE WORKSHEET TO DEFINE YOUR PROSPECT'S **COMFORT ZONE.**

Find the pain

Sorry, the VP of NO isn't interested in what you're selling. At least, that's what he thinks. Satisfied, comfortable people don't change their ways. They change when they have to, and not before. To get the VP of NO to listen, you have to get him out of his comfort zone.

Selling Stars know how to find the pain. Your prospect's pain is a direct result of the way he does things today. Before contacting him, think about his situation. What's wrong with the way he does it today? You believe his current approach needs to change, but he doesn't see it that way. Why should he do it differently?

Will it improve his situation? How? What pain will your solution address? Can you describe it from his point of view? Is the pain likely to be a high priority?

Given all you know about your prospect today, list his top three pains on your worksheet. Write the pain as a statement you might hear from your prospect, for example:

Example:

"I have no time to relax and do the things I really enjoy."

GO TO THE WORKSHEET TO DEFINE YOUR PROSPECT'S **PAIN**.

Questions help identify
& amplify the pain

Once you have identified your prospect's pain, you can't just barge in and tell him. You'll sound like a know-it-all. Think like a buyer: You just met, and suddenly you are an expert in his business, telling him he's an idiot. Even if you're right, this approach will get you the brush-off.

Selling Stars know how to guide prospects through a thinking process, so they come to the right conclusions on their own. The secret is to ask the right kinds of questions.

Open by opening. At this point you want to start a dialogue and provoke thought. Use only open questions. Here are three kinds of questions you can use:

Identifying questions are open-ended, to help you find and prioritize issues:

"*What* keeps you up at night?"

"*What* are your customers' most common complaints?"

Developing questions deepen and broaden your understanding of the issue:

"*What* do you do when this happens?"

"*How* often does this happen?"

"*Who* else is affected?"

Impact questions drive your message home, pointing out the consequences of inaction:

"*If* you keep doing it that way, what will be the result?"

"*What* will happen if this issue isn't addressed?

Develop your pain questions

What questions you can use to identify and develop your prospect's pain? On your worksheet, take a minute to think through the questions you will ask the VP of NO.

Example:

Pain: "I have no time to relax and do the things I enjoy."

Identifying question:

"*What* kinds of things do you like to do in your spare time?"

Developing questions:

"*How* often do you get to do that?"

"*Why* don't you get to do it more frequently?"

"*How* often do things like that get in the way?"

Impact question:

"*How* does that affect your relaxation time?"

Use your questions to find, prioritize and amplify your prospect's pains. By the time he answers your impact questions, he should acknowledge that the current conditions are no longer acceptable. By this time he should look different: decidedly uncomfortable, and a little more open to further conversation. Guess what? He's not the VP of NO anymore. Your questions have transformed him.

Meet the VP of OW.

GO TO THE WORKSHEET TO DEVELOP YOUR PROSPECT'S **PAIN QUESTIONS.**

The VP of OW

The VP of OW is not happy about the current situation. Not happy at all.

"This won't do," he says. "Things need to change around here, and fast."

He clearly sees there's a problem, but, unfortunately for him, he's not sure what to do about it. He's not even sure that it's possible to make things better. That's where you come in.

OW opens the door to new thinking. Now that you've answered your prospect's first question,

"Why should I care?"

I bet you think he's ready to hear about your solution, right? WRONG! He's not ready yet. It's too soon! Remember, he just discovered that he's got a problem. The VP of OW has another question:

"What's in it for me?"

Develop a shared vision

It's time to forget everything you know about your solution. Why? Because the hard truth is:

The buyer doesn't care about your solution.

Difficult as it is to accept, he doesn't care how many amps, bytes, bits or horsepower you can deliver. He cares about what your solution will do for him. He cares about results.

It's time to develop a vision of a brighter future. A future where his pain is a thing of the past. Where he gets the results that he wants. A goal, that you and the VP of OW can share and begin to move toward: A goal that he will need your help to reach. And you will develop this vision together.

Features are facts.
Benefits are results.

Selling Stars understand the difference
between features and benefits, and when
to talk about which.

Benefits are things that customers value. A
hamburger's benefits are that it tastes good
and it fills you up. A benefit is a result.

Features are the specific attributes that deliver
that value. A hamburger's features are the
all-beef patty, bun, lettuce, pickles and onions.
A feature is a fact.

Buyers don't care about features until they
understand the benefits. In other words, all the
pickles and onions in the world won't make a
difference unless the burger tastes good.

For each of the three pains you have identified,
write down a benefit on your worksheet. A true
benefit will usually be almost directly opposite
to the corresponding pain.

Example:

Pain: "I have no time to relax and do the things
I really enjoy."

Benefit: "I have more time for relaxation and
enjoyment."

Describe the benefits you can offer to the
VP of OW, and then ask how they sound.
If your prospect's face brightens and his
demeanor seems more hopeful, he's not
the VP of OW anymore.

Get ready to meet the VP of WOW.

GO TO THE WORKSHEET TO DEFINE YOUR PROSPECT'S **BENEFITS**.

The VP of WOW

The far-off look in your prospect's eyes, and the smile on his face, tell you that you are in the presence of the VP of WOW. He can see the future, and it looks good!

"I get it!" he says. "WOW, this is fantastic!"

You've answered two of his toughest questions:

"Why should I care?" and "What's in it for me?"

He's so excited that he starts painting a picture of the rosy future where everything's perfect and nothing ever goes wrong. His eyes start to get all misty...

WOW points the way.

As the VP of WOW continues to contemplate this beautiful future, he pauses. His face takes on a shrewd, thoughtful look. He asks you, "Is this practical? Is it realistic?"

But what he's really wondering is,

"Why you and not somebody else?"

Before taking action, the VP of WOW must believe that your vision is realistic and achievable, and that you are the one most uniquely qualified to solve his problem.

Features block competitors

Features are practical and realistic because they are facts. They appeal to your prospect's rational side because they relate directly to the product or service, as opposed to his personal feelings. Typically there are far more features than there are benefits. You will be tempted to show off your detailed product knowledge and go into a laundry list of features unique to your solution.

Don't do it!

Your prospect's eyes will glaze over and his face will turn to stone. This is one of the most common mistakes in selling. Think like a buyer! Spewing features is like going on a date and spending too much time talking about yourself.

Selling Stars pick their features carefully – the best features are the ones that only you can offer. Now that you have opened the door with OW, and pointed the way with WOW, you are more vulnerable to competition. Think about it: Your prospect is excited about the vision, but has no reason to make you his first choice.

Pick features that only you can offer, or that none of your competitors can beat. Whenever possible, use the word only – the most powerful "feature word" there is.

Pick your features carefully

For each benefit, write down one significant and competitive feature of your product or service that makes it easier to believe that you are capable of delivering that benefit.

Example:

Benefit: "I have more time for relaxation and enjoyment."

Feature: "The **only** weekly planner custom-designed specifically for you, according to your personal priorities."

After you describe the unique features of your solution, the ones that only you can offer, the VP of WOW nods thoughtfully. He becomes very quiet and looks at the floor. When he looks up again he gives you a skeptical, questioning look.

Get ready to meet the VP of NOW.

The VP of NOW

Suddenly your prospect has become a hard-nosed realist. He starts firing questions at you:

"How does it work?"

"How much does it cost?"

"How will it affect me?"

"What will I need to do differently?"

"Will I need to learn new things?"

It's a little disconcerting, but these are clear signals that your prospect is getting ready to buy. You've answered the questions

"Why should I care? What's in it for me?" and "Why you and not somebody else?"

NOW gives reasons to buy.

But he needs a little more information. After all, you're asking him to take a big leap into the unknown. He needs to understand it a bit more concretely. If he's going to leave his comfort zone, he has to be able to see what his new world will look like.

What he really needs to know is,

"How do I get there from here?"

Make it as easy as 1-2-3

Selling Stars know how to make the future feel concrete, making it easier for their prospects to take that first, most difficult step.

The VP of NOW is seriously considering your solution. He is so serious, in fact, that he has begun to ask himself some very specific questions: "What will I need to do differently? Will it be hard to learn? Will it be hard to use? Will it make my life more complicated?

The secret is to break down this giant leap into a few easy steps. You need to make it as easy as 1-2-3, just like stepping stones make it easier to cross a stream.

Define your process

On your worksheet, write a simple, three-step process that makes using your product or service as easy as 1-2-3.

Example:

1. *First,* we sit down with you to discuss what you value most in life and work.

2. *Next,* we examine weekly activities and compare them with your values.

3. *Finally,* we work with you to create a customized personal planner that will help you achieve your goals.

Now you're getting dangerously close to decision time, and the VP of NOW knows it. Ask him: "So, what do you think?"

The VP of NOW takes a deep breath. Brace yourself.

You're about to meet the VP of HOW.

The VP of HOW

You know that feeling when you are about to leave your house to embark on a long trip? You think "What have I forgotten?" You walk around the house, checking to be sure all the doors are locked and windows closed. Somehow, you can't shake the uneasy feeling that you've forgotten something. Maybe you even wonder for a moment whether this trip was so important after all.

Everyone has this feeling when they are about to leave their comfort zone. The VP of HOW feels like that, right now. Before he makes a final decision, he wants to feel certain he's not making a mistake – and his intuition is whispering, "Play it safe."

What are the risks? He wonders. What's the worst-case scenario? Can I go back if I change my mind later? What if I am wrong?

This is why people offer money-back guarantees – it makes it easier for prospects to make it past this critical stage.

HOW makes the future feel safe.

Your prospect is about to ask you some difficult questions. Questions you would probably rather not have to answer. What he really wants to know is,

"Can I trust you?"

Turn objections on their head

What are the questions you most dread hearing from your prospect? The VP of HOW will be sure to ask them.

Selling Stars know that these questions are not rational but emotional. They are a defense mechanism. The substance of your answers is not really the issue. He may not realize it himself, but your prospect is defending his comfort zone! He is watching your face and body language to determine if you are trustworthy.

Confidence is the key. Confidence comes when you have thought through the issues in advance – when you have anticipated the questions and practiced your responses beforehand. Watch your body language. Lean or step forward into the objection. Give your answer in a confident and straightforward manner. This is a lot harder than it sounds, and it takes practice to do it well. But Selling Stars do it.

If he asks a question that has you stumped, pull out an index card or small pad of paper. Take your time. Write down the objection carefully. Read it back to him to make sure you have it right. Tell him that it's a great question, and promise to look into it.

WORST-CASE

RISK

COLD FEET

NO

JACKPOT

PLAY
★ CAN I ★
TRUST YOU??

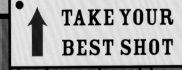
TAKE YOUR
BEST SHOT

Anticipate the toughest objections

The most common way to answer an objection is to turn it on its head. Can you turn a weakness into a strength? With a little thought and creativity, most negatives can be turned into positives. "You're too small" can be turned into "Yes, we're small — much more flexible than big, bureaucratic companies. When you call us on the phone you get a real person."

On your worksheet, write down the three objections you dread hearing the most. Next to them, see if you can craft an answer that turns the objection on its head.

Example:

Objection: "That sounds pretty straightforward. Couldn't I just do this myself?"

Answer: "You have made it pretty clear how frustrated you are by this situation. If you were going to do this for yourself, don't you think you would have done it by now?"

Let the VP of HOW unleash his volley of questions. Listen, empathize with his concerns, and answer the objections thoughtfully. If you are confident, the questions will soon subside. When he's finished, ask "Is there anything else?"

If there is, continue to answer until there are no more objections. When you have finished, get ready to meet the VP of GO!

The VP of GO!

The VP of GO is a pretty nice guy compared to his predecessors. He's got at least three reasons to buy, and he can't really think of any reason not to. He understands the risks and has weighed them against his potential reward.

He has put you through the buying gauntlet, and you have answered every question he has thrown at you:

"Why should I care?"

"What's in it for me?"

"Why you and not somebody else?"

"How do I get there?" and

"Can I trust you?"

He's ready to decide. Still, it's a big step and it's pretty scary.

GO is the moment of truth.

The VP of GO has one final question before he says yes:

"What's the first step?"

Close with three options

You already know what the first step is, don't you? Remember the WHODO? The first step is your call to action, the thing that you want him to DO. He knows it too. You both know.

Although closing is the end of your selling process, it's also a beginning – the beginning of a relationship. Make the first step as easy as possible. Lay out the process – it should already be familiar, because you discussed it in detail with the VP of NOW. The only difference is that now you will secure the buyer's commitment by defining – and getting agreement to – a schedule of events, beginning with the first step: his commitment to proceed.

Selling Stars know that the majority of people, when given a choice between three options, will choose the more moderate middle path.

Offer the VP of GO three choices: a small, medium, and large commitment. Rather than deciding between yes and no, he will then be faced with a different decision: Which option is best? Most likely, he will take the middle option.

Your closing options

Start with your call to action and, on your worksheet, define two more "first step" options for your prospect. One should offer more value for a higher initial commitment. This is called an **upsell**. The other should offer less value for a lower initial commitment. This is called a **downsell**.

Expect the majority of prospects to choose the middle way, but be ready to deliver the other two.

Example:

Call to action: Sign up for my time management seminar

Upsell option: Engage me as your personal time management coach

Downsell option: Take my time management assessment test

Now that you've gone through each stage of the buying process, you're ready to take a look at the Selling Star: a simple tool to help you keep everything in your head.

GO TO THE WORKSHEET TO DEFINE YOUR **CLOSING OPTIONS**.

The Selling Star

The Selling Star is an easy way to help you remember the stages between NO and GO in the correct order. From feeling firm and definitive at the beginning (NO) and end (GO) of the process, to wavering as his comfort zone becomes less comfortable, swinging between emotional and rational states – no wonder your prospect finds big buying decisions so stressful!

As you open the sales process, your prospect is firmly in the NO camp.

NO is the comfort zone

OW opens the door to new ideas

WOW points the way

NOW gives reasons to buy

HOW makes the future feel safe

GO is the moment of truth

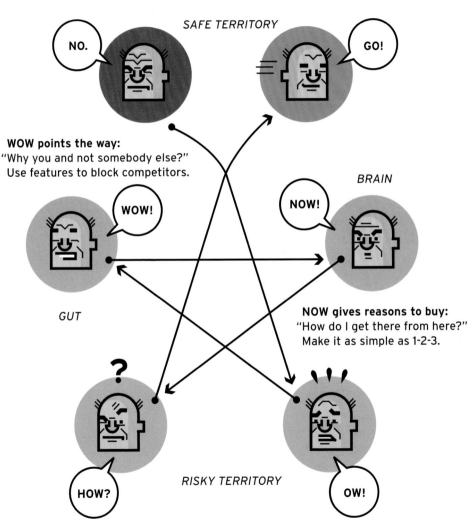

FOUR PRINCIPLES

Think like a buyer

Listen to learn

Open by opening Close by closing

Master the art of asking

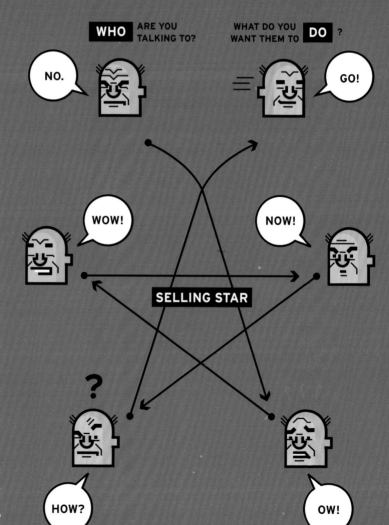

Review

The WHODO

WHO are you talking to, and

What do you want them to DO

The four Selling Star principles:

Think like a buyer

Listen to learn

Open by opening, close by closing

Master the art of asking

The Selling Star

NO is the comfort zone

OW opens the door to new ideas

WOW points the way

NOW gives reasons to buy

HOW makes the future feel safe

GO is the moment of truth

A few more thoughts to get you going

Prepare: Practice till you feel comfortable with your selling story. Practice, practice, practice. Role-play selling situations in advance with a friend or colleague.

Act: The only way to get results is to get started. The sooner you begin, the sooner you will win! Here's a closing question for you:

"Can you think of any reason not to get started today?"

Now that the VP of NO has become the VP of GO, it's time for you to make sure that you deliver everything you promised — but that's another book.

VP OF NO

Further reading

Log on to our website, xplanations.com, where you can subscribe to our newsletter, get updates to the book and check out other goodies like downloads, interactive modules and worksheets.

The purpose of this book is to provide a brief, visual overview of the basics of selling. If you enjoyed this book, you may want to do some further reading. There is a rich literature on the subject of selling, most of which has been written by experienced professionals. Here are a few of the best:

To understand more about the way people make buying decisions, read **Customer-Centered Selling:** Eight steps to success from the world's best sales force, by Rob Jolles.

To learn how executive decision makers think and how to get through to them, read **Selling to VITO:** The Very Important Top Officer, by Anthony Parinello and Dennis Waitley.

Two other excellent books are

Solution Selling: Creating buyers in difficult selling markets, by Michael T. Bosworth, et al, and

New Strategic Selling: The unique selling system proven successfull by the world's best companies, by Stephen E. Heiman and Diane Sanchez

Happy reading!

About the author

Dave Gray is the founder and CEO of XPLANE, the visual thinking company, whose mission is to make complex business issues easier to understand. The ideas in this book are a compilation of best practices and observations gleaned from XPLANE's work with the most effective sales executives and frontline salespeople in some of the world's most successful organizations.

Special thanks

I would like to thank the following people who helped make this idea a reality: Carter Williams of Boeing; Randy Root, founder of Root Learning, Inc.; Peter Gray, principal, Arbor Partners; Peter Evans of Riverdale Partners; Gerhard Gschwandtner, founder and publisher of Selling Power magazine; Mike Berman, principal, CPath solutions; Clay Pew of Draper Fisher Jurvetson; Ted May and the team of visual thinkers at XPLANE who helped turn the concepts into concrete visuals, Brielle Killip for the elegant, clean design, and Jeff Wilson, project manager, for making sure the project was finished on time and under budget. Special thanks are also due to illustrator Dan Zettwoch, who revised the illustrations (and created many new ones) for the third printing.

XPLANATiONs by XPLANE